"Women need their hu[...]sh them. This book provides guidance for husbands to make their prayers meaningful and sustaining for the marriage relationship."

> —LINDA HITCHCOCK, Senior Vice President,
> IndyMac Bank

"Mark's wise insights into Proverbs 31 have raised my awareness of the many ways my wife blesses me and our children. Reading this book has equipped me to pray more specifically for the Lord's continued work in her life."

> —GORDON SPAUGH, Area Executive,
> Branch Banking and Trust Co.

HOW TO PRAY FOR YOUR WIFE

A 31 DAY GUIDE

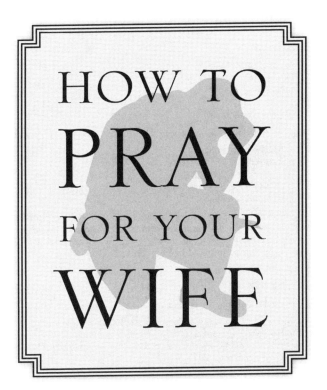

HOW TO PRAY FOR YOUR WIFE

MARK A. WEATHERS

CROSSWAY BOOKS

A PUBLISHING MINISTRY OF
GOOD NEWS PUBLISHERS
WHEATON, ILLINOIS

Cover design: Josh Dennis

First printing 2006

Printed in the United States of America

Library of Congress Cataloging-in-Publication Data
Weathers, Mark A., 1969–
   How to pray for your wife : a 31-day guide / Mark A. Weathers.
      p. cm.
   Includes bibliographical references.
   ISBN 13: 978-1-58134-786-9 (tpb)
   ISBN 10: 1-58134-786-3 (tpb)
   1. Husbands—Religious life. 2. Wives—Religious life. 3. Prayer—
Christianity. 4. Bible. O.T. Proverbs XXXI, 10-31—Criticism,
interpretation, etc. I. Title.
BV4528.3.W43   2006
242'.6425—dc22   2006011337

VP		15	14	13	12	11	10	09	08	07	06
15	14	13	12	11	10	9	8	7	6	5	4	3	2	1

To my mother,

NANCY

whose heart and life have been molded by the gospel
as demonstrated through her unconditional
nurture, love, and hospitality

and

To my wife,

TARA

my perfect partner, lover, and devoted friend,
who has been embraced by the gospel and communicates it
excellently to others in word and action.

CONTENTS

ACKNOWLEDGMENTS

Through writing this book I have come to appreciate that I do not minister in a relational vacuum. So many of my ideas, thoughts, and writings were not birthed solely by me. They are, rather, the result of an intricate weaving contributed over time by family and friends.

Much praise goes to my wife, Tara, who has been the inspiration of this book. I can't express enough thanks for her devoted heart and brilliant theological mind as she read over my evolving manuscript.

Standing applause goes to my parents, Bill and Nancy, whom God has used to model a beautiful marriage that has stood the test of time. Many thanks go to my brother Paul and his wife, Emily, for their excellent help in the editing process. Thanks also go to my brother Steven for his extraordinary thoughts and ideas, which have made the themes of this book stronger.

When I began writing this book, it was not my aim to see it published. Obviously God had other plans. I would like to acknowledge my good friend Dave Vosseller, who ushered my original draft into the hands of Crossway Books.

Praise goes to my mentor and partner in ministry, Stephen Baldwin, whose pastoral influence permeates these pages and is reflected in much of the text.

Acknowledgments

Much appreciation goes to my spiritual family at Providence Presbyterian Church in Concord, North Carolina, for their encouragement and care for me as one of their pastors. It is the Holy Spirit working in their lives that has created such a real and vulnerable community, like none I have ever seen.

I am deeply indebted to my former professors and friends at Covenant Theological Seminary, especially George Van Groningen, Phil Long, and Jack Collins, who instilled within me a passion for Hebrew (still my favorite subject). I also thank Per Almquist, a walking library who was always willing to help me find the source I was seeking.

A final acknowledgment goes to my editor, Lila Bishop, and the folks at Crossway Books for their excellent work of communicating the gospel through publication. (By the way, if you do not have a copy of the English Standard Version in your Bible collection, you are missing out on a great masterpiece of translation.)

INTRODUCTION

*Therefore a man shall leave his father and his mother
and hold fast to his wife,
and they shall become one flesh.*

GENESIS 2:24

I see a unique tree every day while traveling to the church building where I minister. It's a dogwood, and for the majority of the year it looks like any other dogwood in the southeast—slender divided trunk with a bushy green top. But this past spring it caught me off guard as it was coming into full bloom. The tree boasted of both white and pink blossoms intermingled throughout its branches.

It then occurred to me that this dogwood was not a single tree; it was two. Twenty plus years ago two dogwoods—one with white blossoms and one with pink—were planted only inches apart. As these two trees grew, their trunks fused into one, and their branches intertwined with the appearance of being just one tree. Only in the spring, when the vivid blossoms emerge, the tree reveals its uniqueness.

"And the two shall become one flesh." What a beautiful picture this tree is of the mystery of the union created by God between a husband and wife. Two individuals grow together in such a way that their lives fuse together, and their gifts and talents intertwine to create a glorious and unique bouquet for the world to see.

As romantic as this picture is, though, I will be the first to admit that marriage is not always a bed of roses, or dogwood blossoms for that matter. It is true that God has wired men and women differently so as to complement each other, but the world, the flesh, and the devil seek to pervert these differences in order to disrupt unity and to taint intimacy.

In view of this, how do we as men in our God-given roles promote and encourage intimacy in our marriages? The only answer is through the gospel of grace. As children of the kingdom, God loves us unconditionally. He has entered into an everlasting covenant with us—a relationship not based on our works but based on his unchanging love. And since the marriage covenant is designed to reflect the heavenly covenant, the grace that holds us to God (i.e., "cling" as in Genesis 2:24) is the same grace that holds us to each other.

While the covenant is all of grace, we would be wise to study and better understand the uniqueness of masculinity and femininity as expressed in marriage. This is what I seek to do through this journal and study guide.

As a husband, I know it is my responsibility to pray for my wife. Often, though, I do not know the words to use, and I end up feeling that my prayers for her could be more effective. From marriage counseling and pastoral experience, I have met many men who share the same concern. The average Christian man does not know how to pray for his wife. Unfortunately, when we do not know how to pray, we end up not praying at all.

In this process of discovery, I have also found that many Christian women, who are honest enough to admit it, are not enthusiastic about Proverbs 31 because they think that they will never be able to measure up to its seemingly larger-than-life standards. This passage on the "excellent wife" can actually leave them feeling inadequate as wives and mothers. To make matters worse, churches can easily misinterpret this beautiful passage, stripping it of its intended grace, and use it to lay greater guilt on women who are just trying to make it through another day.

It was these thoughts that led me to study this mysterious passage and apply it to husbands for prayer. After an exegetical study of Proverbs 31, which, I might add, was written by a woman, I created this prayer calendar to aid in my prayers for my wife. Having prayed through these requests over the course of several years, I have seen the Lord bless both my wife and my marriage. With this book now in your hands, my prayer is that you and your wife might also experience the Lord's blessing in your marriage. May the Lord give you grace and understanding of his gospel in such a way that your life and marriage stand as a monument to Christ and his glorious church.

HOW TO USE
THIS BOOK

This book is comprised of two parts. The first is an *interactive prayer journal* with thirty-one entries to correspond with the number of days in the month. It is a guide to help you understand and pray for your wife better (or your wife-to-be if you are single). With each day's entry, you will see three things:

1. *Translation*: I have translated each verse at the top of the entry from its original Hebrew into a more literal reading, one that helps to bring out some nuances of the words and phrases.

2. *Explanation*: I have provided a further explanation pointing out significant details about the text and how they point to Christ and the covenant.

3. *Supplication*: Borrowing from the themes in the translation and explanation, I have supplied some suggestions for prayer. As you pray through these items, though, please do not feel limited to my suggestions. Use the translation and explanation as a starting point for your own prayers. This is where the journal becomes *interactive*. You will see spaces where you can write in your own thoughts and prayers.

The second part of this book is a *Study Guide* designed to

help pastors and leaders in their teachings on marriage. It can be used in men's Bible studies, men's retreats, premarital counseling, or discipleship meetings. Feel free to be creative in your implementation of it.

As you read and pray through this devotional, I would like to encourage you to keep a couple of things in mind. First, Proverbs 31:10-31 was originally written as an acrostic poem. This means that the first letter of each verse corresponds to the Hebrew alphabet. This is significant because as an acrostic poem, it was easier to memorize, suggesting that the author wanted these important truths to be embraced.

Second, not only does this passage serve as instructional literature about women, but it also gives great insight into ecclesiology, the study of the church. God created marriage between a man and woman to be a physical picture of the spiritual union between Christ and his bride, the church. As you work through the deep truths of redeemed femininity, my prayer is that you will not only appreciate how your wife is constructed, but that you might also acquire greater insight into the role and mission of the church.

May these deep truths assist your prayers, and may your wife and you be encouraged by God's grace as you grow in intimacy with the Lord and with each other. As you find yourselves embraced by grace, may your marriage become a beautiful reflection of the gospel for the world to see.

He who does not believe in God will not believe in God's people either. But he who has come to believe in God's people will have his eyes opened to the glory of God, even if he was unable to see it before. Only the masses of simple, humble people and their growing spiritual power will be able to convert the atheists. . . . And what good is the Word of Christ without an example? A nation is lost without the Word of God, for every human soul thirsts for the good and the beautiful.

Fyodor Dostoevsky,
The Brothers Karamazov

PROVERBS 31:10-31
(ESV)

¹⁰ An excellent wife who can find?
She is far more precious than jewels.
¹¹ The heart of her husband trusts in her,
and he will have no lack of gain.
¹² She does him good, and not harm,
all the days of her life.
¹³ She seeks wool and flax,
and works with willing hands.
¹⁴ She is like the ships of the merchant;
she brings her food from afar.
¹⁵ She rises while it is yet night
and provides food for her household
and portions for her maidens.
¹⁶ She considers a field and buys it;
with the fruit of her hands she plants a vineyard.
¹⁷ She dresses herself with strength
and makes her arms strong.
¹⁸ She perceives that her merchandise is profitable.
Her lamp does not go out at night.
¹⁹ She puts her hands to the distaff,
and her hands hold the spindle.
²⁰ She opens her hand to the poor
and reaches out her hands to the needy.

²¹ She is not afraid of snow for her household,
for all her household are clothed in scarlet.
²² She makes bed coverings for herself;
her clothing is fine linen and purple.
²³ Her husband is known in the gates
when he sits among the elders of the land.
²⁴ She makes linen garments and sells them;
she delivers sashes to the merchant.
²⁵ Strength and dignity are her clothing,
and she laughs at the time to come.
²⁶ She opens her mouth with wisdom,
and the teaching of kindness is on her tongue.
²⁷ She looks well to the ways of her household
and does not eat the bread of idleness.
²⁸ Her children rise up and call her blessed;
her husband also, and he praises her:
²⁹ "Many women have done excellently,
but you surpass them all."
³⁰ Charm is deceitful, and beauty is vain,
but a woman who fears the LORD is to be praised.
³¹ Give her of the fruit of her hands,
and let her works praise her in the gates.

DAY 1:
SECURITY

PROVERBS 31:10A

An excellent wife . . .

EXPLANATION

The original author of Proverbs 31 chooses an interesting adjective to introduce us to the woman of excellence. Instead of *graceful* or *careful*, which we might expect, she uses a strong word more closely related to battle imagery than to femininity. Some of the meanings attached to the word *excellent* are "valiant," "mighty," "fearless," "strong," and "morally worthy."[1]

In my experience as a pastor I have found that one of the universal characteristics of women is their desire for security. Simply put, a woman's biggest nightmare is to feel insecure and abandoned. Look at the story of Cinderella, or consider the books and movies women love, and you'll see that in every woman is a girl waiting to be rescued and protected by her man. The bottom line is, *women want to feel safe*. But from where should true security come?

Ultimate security comes from God and is provided by the gospel. Christ, our Head, fought to rescue us from death, and he promises his presence for eternity.[2] In addition to looking to Christ for ultimate rescue and security, women look to their husbands. As husbands, we are the heads of our wives,[3] and it is our calling to provide security for them in the same way that Christ provides for his bride.[4] We do this by creating an atmosphere where our wives (and children) can feel safe and secure. When done according to God's design, our marriages become things of beauty that point others to the glorious gospel.

As God demonstrates his love for us by guarding and defending us, and as we demonstrate the same love for our wives, an atmosphere of safety is created, an arena where a woman can come to life. Within a safe environment she can more easily shed her fears and insecurities and thus be freed to express the image and glory of God in her femininity.

A man is made to display strength, and a woman is made to respond to it. Husbands display their strength when they tenderly direct it toward their wives and fiercely direct it toward anything or anyone that would harm them. Such strength is redemptive and life-giving, and it provides the security a wife needs to be strong.

SUGGESTED PRAYER

1. Lord, set my wife free as a redeemed daughter, and restore in her your image so that she might become a strong and mighty woman.
2. Enable my wife to trust in you that you might deliver her from fears and insecurities that haunt her.
3. Enable me to be a husband who provides security to my family just as you provide security for your people. Help me to point my family to you through my words and actions.

JOURNAL

Are there specific insecurities with which your wife struggles and from which she desires freedom? Write your prayer for her in the space below.

_____

_____

_____

_____

ANSWERS TO PRAYER

How has the Lord answered your prayers as you pray for your wife in this area? When was the last time you admired your wife's fortitude? Include it here.

Date: _____ Answer: _____

_____

Date: _____ Answer: _____

_____

Date: _____ Answer: _____

_____

Date: _____ Answer: _____

_____

DAY 2:
TREASURE

PROVERBS 31:10B

. . . who can find?
Her value is far above jewels.

EXPLANATION

After introducing us to a mighty and fearless woman (Day 1), the author asks, "Who can find such a woman?" The question alone implies that this type of person is rare. In fact, if found, her value far exceeds that of precious jewels such as diamonds. The Hebrew word for "jewels" here is also the word for "pearls."

It is fascinating that the excellent woman is compared to a priceless gem that has been cut and polished to perfection. Both diamonds and pearls undergo a process through which they are made beautiful. Diamonds are cut and polished with great precision and care by a master artist. Pearls are created as a result of a piece of sand that has been lodged inside an oyster. This marine mollusk secretes a substance that calcifies around the sand, creating a pearl. Zoologists tell us that this process is as painful for the oyster as it is for a woman to give birth. So a carbon rock becomes a priceless diamond, and a common grain of sand becomes a pearl of great price. Also in both cases, an artist transforms the stones into beautiful and valuable jewels.

This process is very much like the transformation of a sinner to a saint, since the process of salvation is performed by the Master Artist and requires his immediate care and attention. Women do not work harder to transform themselves into persons of excellence. Rather they submit to God's dealings as he works upon them through time, experience, and often through pain to make them beautiful testimonies of God's artistry. God admonishes us husbands to both find and behold the emerging beauty within our wives. A diamond in the rough is still a diamond, and a pearl hidden in a rough and ordinary oyster shell is still a pearl. A woman in the process of sanctification is appreciating into a valuable, "hard to find" woman—a treasure worth so much more than the rarest of diamonds. Begin to view her as such, and you'll discover that you'll value her more and more.

Suggested Prayer

1. Lord, help me see that my wife's value is greater than any earthly thing.
2. Enable me to treat her as the "rare find" that she is.
3. Use me to encourage her in your process of sanctification that you are directing.

Journal

Write some of your own prayers in the space below.

_____

_____

_____

_____

ANSWERS TO PRAYER

How has the Lord answered your prayers as you pray for your wife in this area? Relate instances where you have seen your wife grow in grace through painful times.

Date: _____ Answer: _____

_____

Date: _____ Answer: _____

_____

Date: _____ Answer: _____

_____

Date: _____ Answer: _____

_____

DAY 3:
TRUST

PROVERBS 31:11A

Her husband trusts in her fully . . .

EXPLANATION

What does it mean for a husband to place his trust in his wife? Literally expressed, this verse reads, "The heart of her husband trusts in her."

On a surface level the sentence means that the husband relies on and has full confidence in his wife. The image is of a healthy relationship where the husband does not look over her shoulder, micromanage her actions, or criticize her every move. Usually a man who constantly nitpicks in this way does so not because his wife is inept but because he is insecure.

On a deeper level the husband trusts his wife with his very heart. Instead of being aloof or safeguarding his ego, he is willing to be completely vulnerable with her, knowing that she loves him and has been especially designed to care for him. As men, is it safe to place the very core of our heart's trust in a woman, knowing that we might get hurt?[5] The answer is, no, it is not safe. But God does not call us to be safe; he calls us to sacrifice for our wives—even to the point of death.[6]

You display trust in your wife when you are willing to be

real, when you express to her your own fears and struggles, and when you share with her your hopes and dreams. True, there may be times when your wife may not respond in a way you had hoped, or she may hurt you by dousing your dreams with the cold water of reality. In such instances, do not stop trusting in her. Allow her to be used by the Holy Spirit in your process of being restored into the image of God. As the wise king said earlier in the book, "Iron sharpens iron, and one man sharpens another."[7] You and your wife were designed to sharpen each other.

As your heart trusts in hers, it will accomplish several things: 1) it will build up her confidence, 2) it will cause her to feel loved and trusted by you, and 3) it will enhance the intimacy within your marriage.

> It takes great courage to see the world tainted in all its glory and still love it. It takes greater courage still to see it in the one you love.
>
> Oscar Wilde,
> *An Ideal Husband*

SUGGESTED PRAYER

1. Lord, knowing full well that I risk being hurt, show me how to trust in my wife.
2. Allow my wife to feel the trust I have in her, and use me to build up her confidence in the process.
3. Help me not to be defensive and self-preserving when my wife is being used of you. Enable me to listen to her.

JOURNAL

Write some of your own prayers in the space below.

_____

_____

_____

_____

ANSWERS TO PRAYER

Record the times when you have witnessed your wife growing in confidence through your trust in her. Can you recall times where the Holy Spirit has enabled you to "lay down your life" willingly for her? Thank the Lord for his work in your marriage.

Date: _____ Answer: _____

_____

Date: _____ Answer: _____

_____

Date: _____ Answer: _____

_____

Date: _____ Answer: _____

_____

DAY 4:
PROVISION

PROVERBS 31:11B

. . . And he is never lacking in spoil.

EXPLANATION

Today the author uses another battle term: *spoil*. In virtually every instance in the Old Testament this word is used in connection with war. When a city or nation is conquered, to the victor go the spoils. Through the provision of the woman, her husband is never lacking in spoil. The implication is that a valiant woman is fighting for her man.[8]

At face value this does not mean a woman fights all the family's battles and brings home the spoils, while her husband sits around all day, lazily doing nothing. There are many marriages where this is the case, and wives literally "spoil" their husbands. Such men hide passively behind their wives, giving up the reins in all decision-making. In contrast, this verse echoes Genesis 2:18-24, which describes the creation of Eve.

In all the creation, Adam could not find for himself a suitable helper. The phrase "suitable helper" can be translated literally to "helper according to his opposite." Like a left and right hand, the two are equally made but correspond exactly as mirror images. In other words, God created the woman as a helper for the man, and a man to be a helper for the woman—as one hand is a helper to the other. After all, it is not good for man to be alone.[9] Like a faithful general who fights for his king and brings back the spoils, the woman, out of great devotion to her husband, comes to his side and fights with him and for him in the kingdom of earth and in the kingdom of God.

The bottom line is that God designed your wife to complement you. We understand from the context of this verse in its usage of the word *spoil* that there are some things women do better than men. As you think about your wife, what are the things she is better at than you are? The more you appreciate her feminine design, the more you will see her flourish.

SUGGESTED PRAYER

1. Lord, enable my wife to flourish in the ways you have gifted her, and bless her as she provides for the family and me.
2. Knowing that laziness (abdicating responsibility) is a tendency in all men, please guard me from it. Enable me to fight the battles that I'm called to fight and not expect my wife to do it.
3. Thank you, Father, for creating my wife especially for me. Help me to be appreciative of her and never take her for granted.

JOURNAL

Write some of your own prayers in the space below. Also take this time to express your thanks to God for giving you your wife. List things that she does for which you are thankful. Don't forget to tell her.

_____

_____

_____

_____

ANSWERS TO PRAYER

How have you witnessed your wife growing in her concern and provision for the family?

Date: _____ Answer: _____

_____

Date: _____ Answer: _____

_____

Date: _____ Answer: _____

_____

Date: _____ Answer: _____

_____

DAY 5:
REWARDS

PROVERBS 31:12

She shows him good, not evil,
all the days of her life.

EXPLANATION

The phrase "she shows" could also be translated "she rewards." This is to say that the Proverbs 31 woman rewards her husband with good every day of her life. Rewards are usually earned by a certain kind of behavior or performance. But this is not the case here. This verse implies that the woman respects and provides for her husband "whether or not he actually deserves it." This verse is packed with grace! While most wives would be tempted to retaliate evil with evil, the excellent woman never stops being good to her husband.

This graceful action of the woman parallels the apostle Paul's admonition in Ephesians 5 that wives are to respect their husbands just as husbands are to love their wives (Ephesians 5:33). Again the theme is the same. Men are to love their wives even when their wives may not deserve it, and wives are to respect their husbands when they may not deserve it. Such actions must be done not in our own strength but in the grace of God.

DAY 5: REWARDS

The key to Paul's instruction is that women thrive on feeling loved, and men thrive on feeling respected. When loving and respecting are done in God's strength, the marriage becomes a beautiful cyclical dance: The husband shows his wife love by cherishing and protecting her, and the wife gives honor and respect to her husband. When one partner happens to give in to sin and "misses a step," the other does not retaliate but keeps the dance moving forward.

SUGGESTED PRAYER

1. Lord, give me the grace to love my wife always and to provide her with the security she needs.
2. Help me to be a deserving husband my wife can easily respect, and help my wife to show goodness and grace to me even when I don't deserve it.

JOURNAL

Write some of your own prayers in the space below.

_____

_____

_____

_____

_____

_____

_____

ANSWERS TO PRAYER

How has the Lord answered your prayers as you pray for your wife?
Don't forget to thank the Lord for his work of grace in her life.

Date: _____ Answer: _____

_____

Date: _____ Answer: _____

_____

Date: _____ Answer: _____

_____

Date: _____ Answer: _____

_____

DAY 6:
CREATIVITY

PROVERBS 31:13

*She seeks wool and linen and works
in delight with her hands.*

EXPLANATION

In today's verse the excellent woman shows herself to be active; there is nothing passive or weak about her. She *seeks* wool and linen, implying that she either goes directly to the pasture for sheep's wool or that she goes to the market for it. In either case she takes the raw material and gets busy putting it on the loom (Proverbs 31:19 and 24).

The significant phrase in this verse is the attitude with which she works. The excellent woman *delights in* work. For her, the work is not a duty or drudgery; it is something she enjoys. She takes pleasure in the work of her hands.

Throughout the entire book of Proverbs a contrast resounds between the foolish woman and the wise woman. Early in the book we read of wisdom personified. Consider Proverbs 8:30-31, describing wisdom's vantage point: "Then I was beside him, like a master workman, and I was daily his delight, rejoicing before him always, rejoicing in his inhabited world and delighting in the children of man." As God fashioned the world with amazing creativity, we behold the poetic image that he did it all with wisdom. An excellent woman, therefore, is one who rejoices in the diversity of the created world and then seeks to reflect her Creator as she works in great delight beside him.

As your wife goes about her business of creating, whether it be cooking meals in the kitchen, writing at a desk, researching in a laboratory, engineering a project, designing on a computer, or scrapbooking on the dining room table, pray that she would be surprised by joy as she has the opportunity to reflect the Master Artist.

SUGGESTED PRAYER

1. Father, help my wife to find delight in the rhythms and routines of life. Let her feel your smile as she shops, cooks, works, and creates.
2. Give my wife creativity and excitement as she starts new projects. Bless her in her work and hobbies, and use me to encourage and motivate her.

JOURNAL

Does your wife ever think that she lacks creativity, or does she feel uninspired when it comes to creating? Write some of your own prayers in the space below.

_____

_____

_____

_____

ANSWERS TO PRAYER

Have you seen your wife excited about new projects or creations?

Date: _____ Answer: _____

_____

Date: _____ Answer: _____

_____

Date: _____ Answer: _____

_____

Date: _____ Answer: _____

_____

DAY 7: SERVICE

PROVERBS 31:14

She is like trade ships;
she brings her food from a great distance.

EXPLANATION

What a great analogy to describe the excellent woman! In this verse she is compared to a fleet of merchant ships that have sailed a great distance to bring back supplies. In today's culture we could use the analogy of a supply plane, a fleet of eighteen-wheelers, or even a freight train—all of which travel far and wide to carry supplies.

The woman is undaunted in her service of providing for her family. Whether the children are sick or the husband is at work, the woman goes to great lengths to bring them "her bread" (the literal translation). She delights to serve her family.

Regardless of the time or culture, the role of a servant has never been a popular title. Servants have dirty jobs. Servants get no rest. Yet this is how Christ Jesus continually referred to himself: "For even the Son of Man came not to be served but to serve, and to give his life as a ransom for many" (Mark 10:45). The whole drama of Christ's incarnation, death, and resurrection is a picture of God traveling a great distance to give us heavenly bread. The role of a servant, therefore, is a Christlike occupation. As a woman serves, she has the great opportunity to reflect the Savior.

SUGGESTED PRAYER

1. Lord, as my wife serves the family and me, enable her to see that it is a service rendered for you. Let her service be a sweet offering of praise to you.

2. Father, I know that I am not exempt from serving. On the contrary, as the head of this house it is my responsibility to set the example of service. Help me also to serve joyfully so as to reflect you.

3. As I see my wife "travel" to serve me, let me never take it for granted. Remind me to praise her for her selfless service.

JOURNAL

Write some of your own prayers in the space below.

_____

_____

_____

_____

_____

_____

_____

ANSWERS TO PRAYER

How has the Lord answered your prayers as you pray for your wife in this area? Is God transforming her attitude in the realm of service?

Date: _____ Answer: _____

_____

Date: _____ Answer: _____

_____

Date: _____ Answer: _____

_____

Date: _____ Answer: _____

_____

DAY 8: DEVOTION

PROVERBS 31:15

*And she gets up while it is still dark,
and she gives food to her family
and portions to her servant girls.*

EXPLANATION

The day has not even begun, and the woman gets up early to provide for her family and her servants. Having lived in a culture where maids and nannies are employed, I find it ironic that the woman arises first to get the day going. In many cultures it is the servants' job to do this. Yet here we see the woman devoted to serve the servants.

In the seventeenth century there lived a French monk named Brother Lawrence. By his own confession, he was rather clumsy and not too bright. Because of this the other brothers placed him in the kitchen to cook meals where he might not be a bother. It was in the kitchen, however, where Brother Lawrence learned what he called "the practice of the presence of God." In essence, he fell in love with the Savior through humble service to his fellow monks. In the early morning as Brother Lawrence prepared the meal, this was his posture:

Day 8: Devotion

> We can do little things for God; I turn the cake that is frying on the pan for the love of Him, and that done, if there is nothing else to call me, I prostrate myself in worship before Him, Who has given me the grace to work; afterwards I rise happier than a king. It is enough for me to pick up a straw from the ground for the love of God.[10]

What an amazing devotion to God and to his fellow brothers! And yet as amazing as it is, it is possible for all of God's children to feel such love and devotion to God that will then overflow to the family and others.

Suggested Prayer

1. Lord, as my wife humbly serves the family, let her feel your smile and your presence.
2. Father, as my wife devotes herself to you and the family, may she truly worship as she works.

Journal

Write some of your own prayers in the space below.

_____

_____

_____

_____

_____

ANSWERS TO PRAYER

When have you beheld your wife falling in love with the Savior as she goes about her routine duties?

Date: _____ Answer: _____

_____

Date: _____ Answer: _____

_____

Date: _____ Answer: _____

_____

Date: _____ Answer: _____

_____

DAY 9:
BARGAIN-HUNTER

PROVERBS 31:16A

She considers a field and buys it.

EXPLANATION

The excellent woman is a bargain-hunter. She considers buying a field before she actually "takes" it. The word *considers* means that she purposefully contemplates and strategizes a way to secure it, and then she does just that.

Often I have heard men express misunderstandings about their wives' shopping habits. "Why does a woman need to visit ten stores just to buy one pair of shoes?" To us men, who consider ourselves to be practical, women's shopping methods seem to make no sense. But after careful consideration of this verse, it implies that a woman knows exactly what she is doing. Whether it be shopping for the best bargain, meticulously cutting out coupons, or even buying real estate, women are wired to be smart shoppers.

Interestingly enough, in our country more women than men work as real estate brokers.[11] As brokers, they reflect the excellent woman by researching property on behalf of their clients and then presenting it for possible purchase. Women often give business a personal touch, demonstrating that they are gifted in generating trust and showing reliability.[12]

Day 9: Bargain-hunter

Granted some women go overboard, turning shopping into an idol, but the average woman finds joy in the study and strategy of buying. The key is in understanding the purpose in the shopping. The excellent woman devises[13] a plan that will benefit the whole family, as opposed to scratching the itch of the shopping bug. In either case, when it comes to purchases of any kind (especially high-priced items), we would do well to include our wives in the planning process.

Suggested Prayer

1. Lord, I pray that you would grant my wife discernment in all her endeavors and wisdom in all her purchases.
2. Give her joy as she contemplates and considers her future buying.
3. Enable me to encourage her and bless her in her shopping abilities.

Journal

Perhaps your wife has formed some bad habits in spending. How does this passage apply to her? Write some of your own prayers in the space below.

_____

_____

_____

_____

ANSWERS TO PRAYER

How has God answered your prayers in the area of your wife's purchasing wisdom? Has God changed your attitude through a better understanding of your wife's abilities?

Date: _____ Answer: _____

_____

Date: _____ Answer: _____

_____

Date: _____ Answer: _____

_____

Date: _____ Answer: _____

_____

DAY 10:
ENTREPRENEUR

PROVERBS 31:16B

From the fruit of her own hands,
she plants a vineyard.

EXPLANATION

Immediately after buying a field, the excellent woman wastes no time. With her own hands, she plants a vineyard. There are several implications in view here. We can assume that she prepares the field by clearing it of rocks and weeds. She tills the ground, plants the seeds, and erects some type of pergola to which the grape vines will cling. The fact that she creates a vineyard suggests that she may have the ultimate goal of making wine. And all of this is done "from the fruit of her own hands." Whether she has help from her children or from the family servants, we are not told. Nevertheless, the excellent woman initiates the work and executes it.

These aforementioned details are vitally important for us to consider because through them we see that the excellent woman is not afraid to work—and to work hard. It's also safe to assume that just as she works *in delight* at the loom (31:13), she works *in delight* in her new vineyard.

Underlying these actions is a beautiful work ethic. We should enjoy the work that God has ordained for us—especially when it comes to subduing creation. Adam and Eve were given authority to rule over the earth (Genesis 1:28-30). Whether the work is growing a garden, pruning a tree, pulling weeds, or simply mowing the lawn, we are ruling over creation by not letting it get out of control. These are simple things, but they fulfill our purpose as God's representatives on earth, in addition to reflecting the work of our God. As Moses said in Psalm 90:17: "Let the favor of the Lord our God be upon us, and establish the work of our hands upon us; yes, establish the work of our hands!"

SUGGESTED PRAYER

1. Lord, I pray that you would make my wife into a strong and resourceful woman who loves to work and to create.
2. Empower my wife to research new undertakings, follow through with them, and succeed.
3. May she be an example for me to find new delight in my work.
4. Lord, give my wife joy as she "plants seeds" and puts down roots in our community—and as she watches them grow.

JOURNAL

Regardless of how your wife works (at home, full time away from home, part time, etc.), she still works. How does this passage apply to her? Write some of your own prayers below.

_____

_____

_____

_____

ANSWERS TO PRAYER

How have you witnessed God answering your prayers for your wife in regard to her work ethic?

Date: _____ Answer: _____

_____

Date: _____ Answer: _____

_____

Date: _____ Answer: _____

_____

Date: _____ Answer: _____

_____

DAY 11:
STRENGTH

PROVERBS 31:17

*She dresses herself in strength, and
she makes her arms strong.*

EXPLANATION

The excellent woman is strength personified. She puts on
strength like clothing, and she makes her arms strong. Does this
verse mean that she puts on workout gear every day and heads
to the gym to lift weights? Not exactly. This verse appears in the
midst of various activities typical of a resourceful, energetic
woman of the day—namely, of weaving, bringing food, buying, planting, and creating. It is through these activities that
she makes her arms strong. The poet emphasizes her point by
saying the same thing in two different but parallel ways—
namely, that this woman is strong and mighty.

What does this mean in the context of femininity? After
all, are not men supposed to be the strong ones? Without reading masculinity into the woman's disposition, the author rather
depicts the strength of femininity.

To help us understand better the intended strength and
beauty of a woman, we can look at the church. The redeemed
wife is like the church in its role as the bride of Christ. How,

then, does the church show itself to be strong? Answering this question provides insight into the strength of femininity. The church enthusiastically submits to the Lord in fulfilling its call to make disciples.[14] The church is being made holy and beautiful by the Bridegroom.[15] The church tenderly cares for and nurtures the people of God.[16] The church is an ambassador of reconciliation,[17] the sweet aroma of Christ.[18]

Craig Van Gelder puts it this way: As Christ's bride,

> The children of the kingdom are now to participate in this great redemptive drama by plundering the strong man's stronghold. They are to reclaim lost territory by bringing back to right relationship with God what was lost in the fall. The enemy has been defeated and is bound. Although his power still operates, he has encountered someone stronger. Greater is he who is in the children of the kingdom than he who is in the world.[19]

The church is strong because she has been empowered by Christ. Our wives are strong because they have been empowered by Christ too, but in another sense they have been empowered by us, their husbands.

SUGGESTED PRAYER

1. Father, make my wife into a strong and mighty woman, free from insecurity and fear.
2. Allow our marriage to be a miniature example of the church and Christ's love for his bride.

JOURNAL

Are there specific areas where your wife does not feel strong, emotionally or otherwise? In the space below write your prayer for her in these areas.

_____

_____

_____

_____

ANSWERS TO PRAYER

How has the Lord answered your prayers as you pray for your wife in this area? When was the last time you admired your wife's fortitude? Include it here.

Date: _____ Answer: _____

_____

Date: _____ Answer: _____

_____

Date: _____ Answer: _____

_____

Date: _____ Answer: _____

_____

DAY 12:
ARTISTRY

*She sees that her merchandise
is good . . .*

EXPLANATION

Not only is the excellent woman a strong and resourceful entrepreneur (days 10 and 11), but she also creates a great product. She is proud of her work and makes things that are excellent, as opposed to shoddy. Literally translated, the woman "tastes" her produce and sees that it is good (could this be a reference to her making wine from her newly acquired vineyard?). This wording echoes the original creation. After God created the world out of nothing, he looked upon it and saw that it was "good." The woman reflects her Creator through the act of creating things, including products such as wine. In all of her mini-creations, the excellent woman sees that they are good.

In their book *Culinary Artistry*, authors Dornenburg and Page dedicate their writing as follows: "For the original Creator—architect, artist, author, composer, designer, and mastermind of it all."[20] Reflecting on their dedication, Stephen Baldwin writes:

DAY 12: ARTISTRY

Dornenburg and Page . . . understand that putting a fish sign on a menu doesn't make the food good. Rather, when a Christian makes food it ought to look and taste terrific. It should be excellent in every way. They demonstrate this in their cooking as well as writing, which their receiving the 1996 James Beard Book Award for Best Writing on Food recognize. . . . Often we keepers of the story of redemption forget that God is on a mission to redeem *the universe*, and that means the entire world and all we do in it (whether on a cook top, at a keyboard, in a classroom or practice) is a potential canvas for redemption. The Original Creator is doing something much bigger and more holistic than we think when we consider "the church" or "my job." And that should change the way we think about everything.[21]

SUGGESTED PRAYER

1. Lord, whenever my wife undertakes to create something, I pray that she would be proud of it and that it would indeed be excellent.
2. Bless her skill in a way that it might reflect your work by being "good."

JOURNAL

How does Proverbs 31:18a apply to your wife? Write some of your own prayers in the space below.

_____

_____

_____

_____

_____

ANSWERS TO PRAYER

How has the Lord answered your prayers as you pray for your wife in this area?

Date: _____ Answer: _____

_____

Date: _____ Answer: _____

_____

Date: _____ Answer: _____

_____

Date: _____ Answer: _____

_____

DAY 13:
EXCITEMENT

*. . . She does not extinguish her lamp
at night.*

EXPLANATION

Have you ever been so engrossed in a book that you can't put it down, even after your normal bedtime? Or have you ever been so excited about a project that you can't retire for the day because you want to keep on working? If so, then you know what the excellent woman must feel in this verse. We read that she does not extinguish her lamp, possibly implying that she's so excited in creating that she can't go to sleep. She works in joy to complete her project long after the sun has set.

Once again the woman demonstrates a strong work ethic. But in this verse we do not detect even a hint of her working out of a sense of duty. She is not staying up late because she has to finish. She is not cramming for an exam or finishing a project that she waited until the last minute to begin. Instead, she works because she loves to work (and sometimes some of the best work is done when the house is quiet, and all the kids are in bed).

When Jesus's disciples returned with food from a Samaritan

town, they encountered Jesus just after he had spoken to the Samaritan woman. When they encouraged him to eat, he explained his lack of hunger by saying, "My food is to do the will of him who sent me and to accomplish his work."[22] Doing the Lord's work was so fulfilling that it trumped his desire to eat. Jesus was accomplishing the work for which he came, and that supplied nourishment akin to actual food.

As you see your wife become engrossed in and excited about a project that fulfills her calling as a wife, woman, or mother, do you give her encouragement and praise?

SUGGESTED PRAYER

1. Lord, give my wife joy as she works. Help her to know your calling upon her life and her work.
2. Enable me to praise her and be excited about her projects and her many creative works.

JOURNAL

Write some of your own prayers in the space below. Perhaps your wife has lost a sense of purpose. Pray that God would inspire her to create.

_____

_____

_____

_____

_____

ANSWERS TO PRAYER

How has the Lord answered your prayers as you pray for your wife in this area?

Date: _____ Answer: _____

_____

Date: _____ Answer: _____

_____

Date: _____ Answer: _____

_____

Date: _____ Answer: _____

_____

DAY 14:
MULTITASKING

PROVERBS 31:19

*In her hand she holds the distaff, and
her hands grasp the spindle.*

EXPLANATION

In addition to buying real estate, planting a vineyard, and making wine, the excellent woman sews—though "weaves" is more accurate. She gives new meaning to the word *multitasking*. In the image of sitting down at her loom (an ancient weaving machine), she shows herself to be a capable woman who holds it all together.

I have heard many a man say that he appreciated his wife the most when he had to care for the house and kids for an extended period of time. There are too many things to keep up with in the domestic arena: making sure the family is fed, knowing when to take out the trash, stocking the fridge, cleaning, washing, folding, etc. The list goes on to a point that the average man risks blowing a fuse if he has to manage these things full time. Women are generally better built to keep up with details. The same applies beyond the home front. Some women have become successful career women who can lead a board meeting and still keep their children's soccer schedules and birthdays straight. The point is that God has wired women to be excellent multitaskers.

While men may universally agree with these statements, the importance lies in expressing them. Scores of women feel unappreciated by their husbands because they feel more like battered slaves than cherished wives. They do so much and yet are praised so little. Have you taken the time lately to pause from your schedule and praise your wife for her multitasking abilities?

It is also worth mentioning that even though women are wired to multitask, there are still times when they feel overwhelmed. Such overloads can give rise to feelings of failure, anxiety, bitterness, or anger. When a wife gives in to such temptations, a husband's reaction is to withdraw. This is a sinful response. What a woman needs at such times is a strong man who is not afraid to enter the conflict, help her regain perspective, and reassure her that she is loved and appreciated.

SUGGESTED PRAYER

1. Lord, help my wife, who cares for so much on a daily basis, to see herself as of great value to the family.
2. Enable her to hold everything together and not feel overwhelmed at all the pressures confronting her. Show me what I can do to help.
3. Help me to show genuine appreciation for her and never take her work for granted.

JOURNAL

Perhaps your wife feels overwhelmed at times and needs extra encouragement. How can you pray for her to live up to the way God has built her?

_____

_____

_____

_____

ANSWERS TO PRAYER

How has the Lord answered your prayers as you pray for your wife in this area?

Date: _____ Answer: _____

_____

Date: _____ Answer: _____

_____

Date: _____ Answer: _____

_____

Date: _____ Answer: _____

_____

DAY 15:
HOSPITALITY

PROVERBS 31:20A

*She spreads out her
hands to the poor . . .*

EXPLANATION

Verse 20 (spread between today and tomorrow) contains
some rich concepts regarding a woman's merciful heart. The
excellent woman is not solely focused on her family; she has
a big heart for others. She is deeply concerned about the
needs of those who are poor, suffering, and afflicted—the
latter two words are usually connected with the word *poor*.
In her concern, the woman "spreads out her hands" to
receive those who are in need, allowing them to come and
be cared for.

In opening wide her arms to receive the poor, the woman
becomes a beautiful picture of gospel hospitality. The true
meaning of hospitality does not just mean opening up one's
home for entertainment. It implies opening up one's life as a
refuge for the weary, whereby she creates a safe place for the
troubled to find rest.

In our increasingly suburban society, however, I watch as
families retreat to their own homes and blockade themselves

like knights in a castle. A sense of community is eroding as Christians become reluctant to open their doors to host others. In contrast, the hospitality early believers practiced was significant in the formation of the church, and hospitality is still one of the best methods for communicating a message of grace. As Henri Nouwen wrote:

> Hospitality is the virtue which allows us to break through the narrowness of our own fears and to open our houses to the stranger, with the intuition that salvation comes to us in the form of a tired traveler. Hospitality makes anxious disciples into powerful witnesses, makes suspicious owners into generous givers, and makes close-minded sectarians into interested recipients of new ideas and insights. But it has become very difficult for us today to fully understand the implications of hospitality. Like the Semitic nomads, we live in a desert with many lonely travelers who are looking for a moment of peace, for a fresh drink and for a sign of encouragement so that they can continue their mysterious search for freedom. What does hospitality as a healing power require? It requires first of all that the host feel at home in his own house, and secondly that he create a free and fearless place for the unexpected visitor.[23]

SUGGESTED PRAYER

1. Lord, I pray that my wife would be a woman of great compassion for the poor, needy, and afflicted.
2. Give my wife the grace to open her hands to make our home a hospitable refuge for those in need.

JOURNAL

Write some of your own prayers in the space below.

_____

_____

_____

_____

ANSWERS TO PRAYER

How has the Lord answered your prayers as you pray for your wife in this area? When was the last time you were awed by her hospitable heart? Tell about it here.

Date: _____ Answer: _____

_____

Date: _____ Answer: _____

_____

Date: _____ Answer: _____

_____

Date: _____ Answer: _____

_____

DAY 16:
MERCY

PROVERBS 31:20B

And [she] reaches out to the needy.

EXPLANATION

Yesterday's reading described how the excellent woman opens her hands to the poor. The second half of this verse talks about how, with those same hands, she reaches out to the needy. By her own initiative, she seeks opportunities to show mercy. Such action mirrors the Savior, who said while quoting Isaiah:

> *"The Spirit of the Lord is upon me,*
> *because he has anointed me*
> *to proclaim good news to the poor.*
> *He has sent me to proclaim liberty to the captives*
> *and recovering of sight to the blind,*
> *to set at liberty those who are oppressed,*
> *to proclaim the year of the Lord's favor."*[24]

Through this passage, Jesus teaches that true mercy ministry is done through the anointing of the Holy Spirit, as opposed to being generated by human effort. True motive for mercy comes through the enabling of the Holy Spirit, who was sent to lead us in the continuing ministry of Jesus. Put simply, we become Christ's hands and feet to minister in a broken world wrecked by sin. Under the Spirit's anointing, we proclaim good news to the poor; we proclaim liberty to captives; we help the blind to see and proclaim that now is the time of God's favor.

SUGGESTED PRAYER

1. Lord, enable my wife through the power of your Spirit to be Christ's hands and feet to the poor, needy, and afflicted. Give her a heart of compassion.
2. As my wife comes into contact with others who may be in spiritual bondage, use her (and her gifts) to set them free.
3. I pray that you would give my wife wisdom and discernment as she cares for others and that she would know how to create good boundaries.
4. Pray through Luke 4:18-19 (page 83), asking the Lord to make you and your wife instruments of God's mercy through the demonstration of the gospel at work in you.

JOURNAL

Write some of your own prayers in the space below.

_____

_____

_____

_____

_____

_____

ANSWERS TO PRAYER

How has the Lord answered your prayers as you pray for your wife in the area of mercy? Cite some specific times when she has reached out with hands of compassion.

Date: _____ Answer: _____

_____

Date: _____ Answer: _____

_____

Date: _____ Answer: _____

_____

Date: _____ Answer: _____

_____

DAY 17: COVERING

PROVERBS 31:21

*She is not afraid of snow
for her household, because all
of them are doubly clothed.*

EXPLANATION

Once again the excellent woman shows herself to be fearless. Even in the severest of weather she is not afraid because she has doubly clothed the members of her household. Some Bibles render the latter phrase as "clothed in scarlet," which is an optional translation. In either case, the meaning has the same thrust: Because the woman has provided covering for the members of her household, she is not afraid of coming snow.

In this beautiful verse much more is implied than a woman buying (or making) clothes to cover her family adequately. The very redemptive heart of God is reflected in these actions.

In Genesis 3 soon after Adam and Eve had broken God's command by eating of the forbidden tree, they felt guilt for the first time. In their shame they sewed together leaves to cover their nakedness. When God called to them, it was obvious that their shoddy attempt to make themselves presentable to stand before the Lord was insufficient. So God slaughtered an innocent animal, and from its hide he clothed them.[25] Throughout Scripture the same story is told over and over: *God provides covering for his people.* From Adam and Eve all the way to the cross, God was providing clothing for his people so that they could live in his presence forever. The message of the cross shouts aloud that we cannot stand before God dressed in our shoddy attempts at good living. To stand before God requires that we be dressed in the goodness of Christ, whose innocent blood was shed to cover us. Therefore we need not fear in the severest of spiritual weather because we are sufficiently clothed from on high.

Open your eyes to behold the ways your wife prepares for the "heavy weather" that may come and how she is imaging the Lord in providing for the various needs of the family. Pray that she would provide a double portion of all that is needed, both physically in the areas where she works hard and emotionally through her encouragement, support, and praise. Encourage her to see how she reflects the message of redemption in providing sufficient covering for the family.

Suggested Prayer

1. Lord, in the severest of weather (or circumstances), set my wife free from anxiety and fear because you have clothed us with the goodness and righteousness of Christ.
2. Enable my wife to give every member of the house a double portion of provision—both physical and emotional.

JOURNAL

Does your wife ever get frustrated over all that she has to do to care for the family? How can you specifically pray for her in view of this verse?

_____

_____

_____

_____

ANSWERS TO PRAYER

How has the Lord answered your prayers as you pray for your wife in this area?

Date: _____ Answer: _____

_____

Date: _____ Answer: _____

_____

Date: _____ Answer: _____

_____

Date: _____ Answer: _____

_____

DAY 18:
BALANCE

PROVERBS 31:22

*She makes for herself
coverings of tapestry; and linen
and purple are her clothing.*

EXPLANATION

After thirteen verses describing the excellent woman's actions toward others, she finally pampers herself. She makes for her home beautiful coverings of embroidered tapestry, perhaps a carpet or bedspread, demonstrating that she is an able interior decorator. As for her clothing, it is fine linen and purple, an expensive color signifying royalty.

We understand from the whole chapter that the excellent woman has a beautifully balanced life. She takes care of herself but does not neglect her family (31:14). She dresses in regal clothes but is still willing to serve the servants (31:15).

Balance in life is hard to achieve. Some women over-pamper themselves and in their selfishness neglect their families and callings. Self has become their idol, and they worship themselves as those who deserve the best. On the other hand, some women feel guilty any time they seek to rest from life's demands, thus playing the role of the martyr. Such women have assumed too much upon themselves and feel that if they do not do it all, they are failures. This too is self-worship because they want everyone to know how much they slave for the family. In either case, how are women to be liberated from this tension?

John gives the example in John 13 when Jesus took a towel and washed his disciples' feet. Jesus could do this because he knew exactly who he was, where he had come from, and where he was going.[26] "Secure in that knowledge," wrote Edmund Clowney, "he was untouched by the defensiveness of insecure pride. So, too, the knowledge of glory equips us to serve: first as sons in the Son, then as servants in the Servant. With the cry 'Abba, Father' on our lips, we can take the towel as Jesus did. God's grace first saves us and then equips us for service. . . . We serve as we use the gifts of the Spirit. Our ministry is therefore humble service, not selfish manipulation."[27]

As your wife seeks to live a balanced life, help her to know who she is, where she has come from, and where she is going. She is a beloved princess in the kingdom of God, dressed in the very royal robes of Christ.[28]

SUGGESTED PRAYER

1. Lord, guard my wife from idolatry in the form of self-indulgence or self-martyrdom.
2. Help my wife to see herself as a princess who loves life in your kingdom.

JOURNAL

There is much more that can be derived from Proverbs 31:22. Do you have any further thoughts as to how you can pray for your wife?

_____

_____

_____

_____

ANSWERS TO PRAYER

How has the Lord answered your prayers in this area?

Date: _____ Answer: _____

_____

Date: _____ Answer: _____

_____

Date: _____ Answer: _____

_____

Date: _____ Answer: _____

_____

DAY 19:
SIGNIFICANCE

PROVERBS 31:23

*Her husband is known at the city gates
where he takes his seat
with the elders of the land.*

EXPLANATION

When coupled with the whole passage, this verse demonstrates
that the family is well respected in the community. The husband
of the excellent woman is an honored elder who takes his seat
with other wise men as a leader of the city. This group of elders judges the cases brought before the assembly.

God created man as the king and ruler of creation, and he
has wired men to desire honor and respect.[29] If a woman's greatest desire is for security (see Day 1), a man's greatest desire is for
significance.[30] When a man does not feel significant, it negatively
affects his work, his family, and his marriage.

As men, we face several temptations when it comes to feelings of insignificance. First, there is a tendency to find our significance in other things, such as work or pleasure. Second, it
is tempting to blame someone else: "If I feel insignificant, it is
my wife's fault. I deserve to be treated with respect." In either
case, just as women are to seek ultimate security from God,

we must seek ultimate significance from him as well. Even if you were a perfect man who commanded respect, it would still not guarantee that you would receive it. Regardless of how we are treated, our significance must be derived from the gospel. We are created in God's image,[31] and we have been adopted into his family.[32]

SUGGESTED PRAYER

1. Lord, make our marriage (and family) one that is known and respected in the community.
2. Help my wife to know how to show me respect and significance. And even when she doesn't, let me derive my significance from you.
3. Lord, are there "idols" in my life that tempt me to trust in something other than you for my worth? If so, reveal them to me and give me the grace to repent of them.

JOURNAL

Write some of your own prayers in the space below.

_____

_____

_____

_____

_____

ANSWERS TO PRAYER

How has the Lord answered your prayers as you pray in this area?

Date: _____ Answer: _____

_____

Date: _____ Answer: _____

_____

Date: _____ Answer: _____

_____

Date: _____ Answer: _____

_____

DAY 20:
LIGHT

PROVERBS 31:24

She makes linen garments,
which she sells,
and gives belts to the merchants.

EXPLANATION

The excellent woman shows herself to be a light to the world. She makes exquisite articles of clothing, which she then sells to the merchants. The word for merchant is *Canaanite*, signifying that these folks were foreigners. By selling and delivering needful things, the excellent woman displays a concern for those who do not yet know the God of Israel, and she gladly engages in commerce with them.

By giving the Israelites the land of Canaan as an inheritance, God had set his chosen people in a strategic position. In this "street corner" location, anyone traveling between Asia Minor and Egypt had to pass through Israel. God's design in this was that his treasured people might be a conspicuous light to the nations.[33] Throughout the Old Testament, however, we read that Israel misunderstood the vision God had for them. Either they fully embraced the religions and idols of the surrounding nations, or they looked down upon them with an elitist attitude. In either case, they were not bringing the light of the gospel.[34]

Within the church we fall victim to these two sins of Old Testament Israel. Either we embrace the idols of our culture and therefore look no different from the world around us, or we huddle together in Christian enclaves, condemning the world's actions from a safe distance. Both behaviors are wrong and stand opposed to the gospel that Christ wants us to uphold. The excellent woman is not afraid to stand and work among foreigners or to get to know them by name. In so doing, she displays God's compassion for a lost world. Jack Miller sums this up best in his book *Outgrowing the Ingrown Church*:

> [God's] purpose is a grand redemptive one, the forming of a completed new people of God out of the rubble of fallen mankind. In the Scriptures this completed church is called "the bride," "the wife of the Lamb," who upon His return will be made perfectly spotless and complete. But the church herself is more than the goal. She is also the vehicle, the instrument, for gathering in the people of God. Christ has no other agency for accomplishing this work. . . . It is commissioned to act as Christ's sole representative for carrying the gospel to the nations. Thus the Great Commission assigns the church a task, a missionary purpose, as the means for accomplishing Christ's broader purpose, the ingathering of the whole people of God.[35]

Suggested Prayer

1. Lord, make my wife into a compassionate woman who continually shines your grace.
2. Give my wife a fearless heart that seeks to display your gospel within the world.

JOURNAL

Write some of your own prayers in the space below.

_____

_____

_____

_____

ANSWERS TO PRAYER

How has the Lord answered your prayers as you pray for your wife in this area?

Date: _____ Answer: _____

_____

Date: _____ Answer: _____

_____

Date: _____ Answer: _____

_____

Date: _____ Answer: _____

_____

DAY 21:
MAJESTY

PROVERBS 31:25A

Strength and majesty are her clothing.

EXPLANATION

This verse is very similar to verse 17 where we read of the woman dressing in strength. Here, though, the author uses a new word: *majesty*. Other possible synonyms include dignity, honor, and glory.

Considering the author of Proverbs 31, this verse stands out as a beauty. Verse 31:1 indicates that King Lemuel's mother wrote this passage. It is thought that Lemuel was another name for King Solomon,[36] the overall author of Proverbs. If this is true, the original author of Proverbs 31 would be none other than Bathsheba, the wife of King David.[37]

Whether or not Bathsheba originally penned these words, we can, nevertheless, learn much from a brief overview of her life. When she first appears on the biblical scene, Bathsheba is caught immodestly bathing upon her roof in full view of the palace.[38] Later we might get the impression that her husband, Uriah, was more devoted to his work than to his wife,[39] possibly suggesting that all was not well within their marriage. Bathsheba and David fall into an adulterous relationship that leads to a pregnancy, and David stages the murder of her husband. Given these details, Bathsheba does not seem to be a woman who personifies majesty or dignity.

In spite of Bathsheba's sin and culpability in her affair with David, her life majestically stands as a tower of grace. How can that be? The Lord stepped into the situation and took actions to redeem it. David and Bathsheba received pardon, and God granted them a son, whom they named Solomon. And it was Bathsheba who became one of the ancestors of Christ.[40] It is tempting to think that had the couple not sinned, the line of Christ would have been broken. But this is not the case. God sovereignly worked through David and Bathsheba's failings to accomplish his set purpose. Not only is Bathsheba mentioned in Matthew's genealogy of Christ, but he also includes three other women who stand out as majestic pillars of grace: Tamar, the daughter-in-law of Judah who tricked him into fathering a son; Rahab, the former prostitute of Jericho; and Ruth, the widowed foreigner of Moab.

Whatever history your wife brings into your marriage, know that we serve a God who not only redeems the past, but he also uses it for the advancement of his kingdom. As your wife puts her faith in the gospel, pray that she might stand as a majestic tower of God's amazing grace.

SUGGESTED PRAYER

1. Lord, cause my wife to stand as a tower of grace as she looks to you for her righteousness, and help her to become a woman of majesty and dignity.

2. When my wife is temped to despair because of her past mistakes, help her to recall the gospel that has both saved her and is currently restoring her.

JOURNAL

Does your wife struggle with feelings of disgrace or shame because of her past? Write some of your own prayers specifically for her.

_____

_____

_____

_____

ANSWERS TO PRAYER

How has the Lord answered your prayers as you pray for your wife in this area?

Date: _____ Answer: _____

_____

Date: _____ Answer: _____

_____

Date: _____ Answer: _____

_____

Date: _____ Answer: _____

_____

DAY 22: LAUGHTER

PROVERBS 31:25B

And she laughs at the days to come.

EXPLANATION

The author of Proverbs 31 uses a colorful verb in this verse to describe the excellent woman. "She laughs" can also be translated to "she plays." In other words, this regal woman can sing, dance, and laugh. Not only is she strong and majestic; she is a carefree woman who knows when to "let her hair down."

One of the most attractive things to a man is a woman who is free-spirited and seeks to live life to the fullest.[41] Such a woman is unencumbered by the unrealistic pressures of the outside world because she stands confident in her inner beauty. She knows when to be proper and when to cut loose. She beats to the tune of heavenly drums and attracts others to her ongoing party.

I believe that within each woman is a yearning to laugh. Women's magazines still maintain that the attribute a woman is looking for most in a man is a sense of humor. This should tell us that a woman longs to feel safe in the arms of a man who will keep life in perspective by not taking everything so seriously and by leading them into laughter. Understood from the sovereignty of God, we can all laugh and play as we look to the future because we know the One who orchestrates all things. A woman in such a relationship knows not just *who* she is but *whose* she is.

SUGGESTED PRAYER

1. Lord, make me into a man who provides safety and security for my wife on all levels: emotional, spiritual, and physical.
2. Lord, whenever I fall victim to my own insecurities, thereby refraining from leading my wife in the way she needs, enable her to cling to you in faith.
3. Lord, never let my wife lose the heart of a child. Let her laugh, dance, and play because her confidence is in you.

JOURNAL

Write some of your own prayers in the space below.

_____

_____

_____

_____

_____

_____

_____

ANSWERS TO PRAYER

How has the Lord answered your prayers as you pray for your wife? Can you recall recent times when you have seen your wife laughing?

Date: _____ Answer: _____

_____

Date: _____ Answer: _____

_____

Date: _____ Answer: _____

_____

Date: _____ Answer: _____

_____

DAY 23: WISDOM

PROVERBS 31:26A

She opens her mouth with wisdom.

EXPLANATION

Whenever the excellent woman opens her mouth, she speaks with wisdom. Throughout the book of Proverbs, wisdom is colorfully portrayed. Wisdom is a tree of life (15:4). Wisdom brings healing (12:18). Wisdom is an edifying builder (14:1). The caricature of wisdom is beautifully diverse, but one of its common themes is that it is life-giving.[42] In the context of this verse, the excellent woman uses her mouth to build up, to heal, and to promote instruction.

In contrast to the wise woman, the woman of folly is loud and ignorant.[43] Instead of building up, she tears down. Instead of communicating life-giving instruction, she promotes death. This contrast of wisdom versus folly teaches us that the tongue can either be an edifying tool or a destructive weapon.[44]

Since women are generally better communicators than men, they are more susceptible to the sins of the tongue such as gossip or slander. Both gossip (speaking incriminating *truth* about someone) and slander (speaking incriminating *lies* about someone) are destructive. The motivations for these deadly sins of speech are subtle: the lust for power and control over someone else's reputation or the feelings of insecurity that drive one to tear down another in order to feel good about self.

Seen from wisdom's perspective, though, the excellent woman's tongue operates out of love. If you love someone, you will care for his or her reputation enough not to defame it. If you love someone, you will seek to build the person up through encouragement, praise, and instruction (and even sometimes through a loving rebuke).

As you listen to your wife, do you discern her communication to be motivated by love, resulting in life-giving words, or do you perceive them to be fueled by insecurities, resulting in destructive speech? Pray for her as she struggles in these areas.

SUGGESTED PRAYER

1. Father, I pray that your love would so fill my wife's heart that she would use her tongue to speak edifying words of wisdom to me, to the family, and to our community and church.

2. Lord, you know my wife's heart. Please deliver her from insecurities that would motivate her to use her tongue in a destructive way.

3. Give me the strength to love her enough to confront her if she sins in this area, and give her a wise and receptive heart to hear it.

JOURNAL

Does your wife struggle in this area? Write some specific prayers of your own in the space below.

_____

_____

_____

_____

ANSWERS TO PRAYER

How has the Lord answered your prayers as you pray for your wife's heart and speech?

Date: _____ Answer: _____

_____

Date: _____ Answer: _____

_____

Date: _____ Answer: _____

_____

Date: _____ Answer: _____

_____

DAY 24: GRACE

PROVERBS 31:26B

And the law of grace is on her tongue.

EXPLANATION

A literal translation of verse 26 reads, "She opens her mouth with wisdom and speaks of the law of grace." I want to mention two things about this beautiful phrase, "the law of grace."

Law: The law is something we live by. Laws govern our lives and allow us to live at peace with one another. The law is something we are to submit to lest we endanger others and ourselves. In this verse, as the woman speaks, she proclaims the law of grace, implying that not only does she live by it, but also she communicates it to others. The law of grace governs her life.

Grace: In this verse the writer uses the most famous Old Testament word for grace. In Hebrew it's pronounced *hêsed*, and it almost always refers to God's steadfast love for his people (see Psalm 136, which has the repeated refrain "for his steadfast love endures forever"). The implication is that the woman trusts in the grace of her Lord to an extent that she cannot keep silent about it. Her God loves her with an everlasting love, and she loves others with the same grace. I think the apostle Paul sums it up best when he wrote to Titus saying:

> *For the grace of God has appeared, bringing salvation for all people, training us to renounce ungodliness and worldly passions, and to live self-controlled, upright, and godly lives in the present age, waiting for our blessed hope, the appearing of the glory of our great God and Savior Jesus Christ, who gave himself for us to redeem us from all lawlessness and to purify for himself a people for his own possession who are zealous for good works.*[45]

SUGGESTED PRAYER

1. Lord, let the doctrine of grace rule my wife to the point that she talks about it to others.
2. Help her to understand your grace—that she is your dearly loved child not because of what she has done, but because of what Christ has done.
3. Purify my wife as your own possession that she would be zealous for good works.

JOURNAL

Write some of your own prayers in the space below.

_____

_____

_____

_____

ANSWERS TO PRAYER

How has the Lord answered your prayers as you pray for your wife? Have you heard her remarking lately about how amazing God's grace is?

Date: _____ Answer: _____

_____

Date: _____ Answer: _____

_____

Date: _____ Answer: _____

_____

Date: _____ Answer: _____

_____

DAY 25:
WATCHWOMAN

*She watches over
the way of her household.*

EXPLANATION

The excellent woman gives new meaning to the statement, "The woman is the manager of the home." Here we find her watching over all the doings, travels, and ways of the household.

The Hebrew verb for "watches" also appears as a noun throughout the Old Testament as "watchman." The watchmen were the soldiers who stood guard over the city walls throughout the day and night, watching for a possible attack on the city. When they perceived a potential threat, they notified the military and the civilians so that defensive action could be taken.

In a similar way, the excellent woman stands as a watchwoman over the ways of her household. She observes the comings and goings of each family member, and she is alert to any danger that might invade the domestic arena.

The two greatest complaints that I have heard children voice about their mothers (or husbands about their wives) are that they ask too many questions and that they nag. While interrogating and nagging can, at times, be sinfully overdone, these are two ways a woman fulfills her design as a guardian over her

119

family. Asking questions is her way of saying, "To help keep you safe, I need to know where you are going, what you'll be doing, and when you'll be home." Nagging is her way of communicating, "Take action! I'm looking out for the well-being of the family and household. So please clean your room. Please fix that leaky faucet, etc."

The bigger picture here is that what the woman does for her family is what God does for his children. Psalm 121 and 139 are beautiful passages that poetically celebrate how God watches over his loved ones.

SUGGESTED PRAYER

1. Lord, help my wife to fulfill her design as a watchwoman of our home. When she sees danger and alerts me to it, enable me to take action as the man of the house and not be critical of her.
2. Help my wife to be vigilant as she seeks to watch over the family. Give her keen insight into the dangers that might infiltrate our home through the television, the Internet, or ideas brought home from school.

JOURNAL

Write some of your own prayers in the space below.

_____

_____

_____

_____

ANSWERS TO PRAYER

How has the Lord answered your prayers as you pray for your wife in this area?

Date: _____ Answer: _____

_____

Date: _____ Answer: _____

_____

Date: _____ Answer: _____

_____

Date: _____ Answer: _____

_____

DAY 26: ACTIVE

PROVERBS 31:27B

. . . And [she] does not eat the bread of slothfulness.

EXPLANATION

As the excellent woman watches over the ways of her household, she is not guilty of slothfulness. Other synonyms of slothfulness include laziness, sluggishness, or idleness. Does this mean that the excellent woman is a work machine, constantly busy and never at rest? The key phrase is that the woman does not "eat the bread of slothfulness."[46] This is to say she does not reap the rotted fruit of laziness; nor does she indulge herself in sluggish behavior. As journalist Henry Fairlie expressed it:

> Sloth is preeminently the sin of omission . . . it is a sin of neglect. We neglect what we ought to do, and especially we neglect our neighbors . . . even to callousness. We pass by on the other side, partly out of pride, of which there is a lot in sloth, but partly out of mere indolence, a laziness of the spirit as well of the flesh. Increasingly in our societies, we barely lift a finger for the poor and the downtrodden. Our technology and our gadgets have freed us from most drudgery, and what do we do with the time that is now available to us? We turn inward and become utterly absorbed in ourselves.[47]

DAY 26: ACTIVE

While it might seem that men tend more often to be guilty of sloth than women, the focus in today's reading is that sloth-fulness can affect women. Just because one is busy does not mean she is not guilty of slothfulness. In our culture, there is an unchecked emphasis on self-actualization. From self-help books to spa retreats, consumers are proselytized to worship them-selves as the center of their universe. Women are praised for their busyness, not on behalf of their families but for themselves. This is at the root of slothfulness. The excellent woman, there-fore, is an active woman who is not self-absorbed. She is a redeemed soul who looks not only to her own interests but to the interests of others as well,[48] especially to those in her household.

SUGGESTED PRAYER

1. Lord, as you work in my wife's heart, guard her from being self-absorbed. Give her a heart that seeks to love and care for those around her.
2. Enable my wife to have the same attitude as that of Christ, caring for the needs and interests of others above those of her own.

JOURNAL

Write some of your own prayers in the space below. Perhaps your wife is too busy and needs to slow down. How would you pray for her in light of Proverbs 31:27b?

_____

_____

ANSWERS TO PRAYER

How has the Lord answered your prayers as you pray for your wife in this area?

Date: _____ Answer: _____

_____

Date: _____ Answer: _____

_____

Date: _____ Answer: _____

_____

Date: _____ Answer: _____

_____

DAY 27: CHERISHED

PROVERBS 31:28

*Her children stand up
and call her blessed;
and her husband praises her.*

EXPLANATION

The family of the excellent woman cannot stay seated about her. The children are crazy about their mother and stand up to remind her how blessed she is. The woman's husband also joins in the praise by boasting of what a great wife he has. The excellent woman is a cherished woman.

One of the most dangerous sports in which a man can engage with a group of his buddies is verbal wife-bashing. Like a belligerent cloud of hungry locusts, a group of men can strip bare and ravage their wives' characters in a fraction of a moment. To a man it may seem like harmless teasing, but every time he makes a joke about his wife in her presence, you can see a sadness appear in her eyes. What may then proceed from her mouth, though, may be a different story. Many a marriage suffers due to a husband's unchecked teasing or complaining about his wife.

The bottom line is that a woman needs to be cherished and loved by her husband.[49] One of the greatest ways to convey your

DAY 27: CHERISHED

admiration for your wife is to communicate it to others in such
a way that she hears it or will hear it later. Such praise makes a
woman beam. If you have children, praising your wife will
strengthen their admiration for her as well; not to mention, it
will also reassure them that even though Dad and Mom sometimes disagree, they still love each other deeply.

SUGGESTED PRAYER
1. Lord, forgive me for the times when I have callously made
   fun of my wife in front of others.
2. Father, help me to praise and cherish my wife. Let her feel
   loved and admired as I seek to use my mouth to build her up.

JOURNAL
Write some of your own prayers in the space below.

_____

_____

_____

_____

ANSWERS TO PRAYER
How has the Lord answered your prayers as you pray in this
area?

Date: _____ Answer: _____

Date: _____ Answer: _____

_____

Date: _____ Answer: _____

_____

Date: _____ Answer: _____

_____

DAY 28: APPRECIATION

PROVERBS 31:29

*"Many women do noble things,
but you go beyond them all."*

EXPLANATION

This verse is in quotes because it should be read as the praise echoed by the husband and children. The family acknowledges that though there may be other women who act nobly, this woman surpasses them all. If you detect a bias here, you understand the theme correctly. In modern times, it might be like seeing several women wearing a shirt that says, "World's Best Mom." Logic tells us that there can only be one best mom. But that is not the point. According to the children and husband, their woman is the best.

When it comes to appreciation, we will praise what we value. If something has depreciated in value, it receives less praise (compare a new car to a used car, for example). In marriages, the tragedy is that when a wife depreciates in her husband's eyes, criticism replaces praise.[50] How does a woman gain appreciation? It is not through working harder. For a woman to increase in value, the value must be given to her by her man. Ultimately, the Lord must transform a man's heart. It is all of grace—and not as a result of our actions—that the Lord loved us and entered into a covenant with us.[51] In the same way, our love for our wives should not be based on their actions, but on the covenant we made with them as we stood and exchanged vows. Eugene Peterson expanded on these themes when he wrote about the Song of Solomon:

> God, delighting in us, festoons his creatures, just as we, when we delight in another, enhance and elaborate the beloved. With the help of a vocabulary learned in the Song [of Solomon] we see God's people (and ourselves) not through the dirty lenses of our own muddled feelings, and not through the smudgy window of another's carping criticism, but in terms of God's word. We never know how good we can look, how delightful we can feel, or how strong we can be until we hear ourselves addressed in love by God or by the one who represents God's love to us. That which in itself is without value acquires value by the fact that it is the object of God's love.[52]

SUGGESTED PRAYER

1. Lord, forgive me for being quick to criticize my wife and reluctant to praise her.
2. Father, I beg you to transform my heart. Renew my passion and appreciation for my wife—not based on her actions but based on my love and commitment to her.

JOURNAL

Are you convicted by today's reflection? Write some of your own mediations and prayers in the space below.

_____

_____

_____

_____

ANSWERS TO PRAYER

How has the Lord answered your prayers in this area? Do you find yourself praising your wife? Have you heard your children praise her?

Date: _____ Answer: _____

_____

Date: _____ Answer: _____

_____

Date: _____ Answer: _____

_____

Date: _____ Answer: _____

_____

DAY 29: IDOL-SMASHER

PROVERBS 31:30A

Elegance is a lie; beauty is vanity.

EXPLANATION

From glamour magazines to soap operas, the world sets a high bar for women. According to our culture, beauty is defined by externals: a pretty face, graceful actions, and a nice figure. In this verse, though, we are given the true definition of beauty, where the author accurately describes what beauty is not. It is not in being graceful and elegant, having all the right moves—that is a lie. Nor is it about possessing a gorgeous face and body, having all the right looks—that is empty.[53] Considering these concepts, both we and our wives need to embrace the magnitude of this verse.

Sin has so perverted the idea of what is beautiful that both sexes can be guilty of idolatry. Women prostrate themselves to the idol of beauty when they compare themselves to the women of fashion. The mirror thus drives women to worship at the altar of the bathroom vanity. We men are just as guilty when we worship the idol of beauty in the form of lust. Whether letting our eyes linger too long on a voluptuous figure or gawking at outright pornography, we show ourselves to be enslaved by a

135

manmade idol. Through such actions we send the message that our wives are lacking in beauty, which can drive them to despair.

As disciples of Christ we need to engage in the spiritual battle of shattering this culturally made idol of beauty. In your prayers, ask the Lord to work in your wife's heart that she would refuse to let culture dictate her idea of beauty. Second, consider this great truth by Bruce Marshall: "The young man who rings the bell at the brothel is unconsciously looking for God."[54] Within our hearts is a desire for what is truly beautiful, and Marshall hits home with this thought, because deep down we are seeking true intimacy. Giving in to the temptation of lust is settling for a cheap imitation of the intimacy that only God can provide. When you are tempted, ask the Holy Spirit to give you a spiritual nudge that will drive you to your knees to seek intimacy with the Father's heart.

Suggested Prayer

1. Lord, help my wife not to compare herself to other seemingly beautiful women.
2. Enable her not to derive her idea of beauty from popular women's magazines, television, or movies. Instead expose their deceit and emptiness.
3. Father, help me to shatter the idol of beauty in my own heart and so build up my wife in her own true beauty and confidence.

JOURNAL

There is a lot to think about in this verse. Write some of your own prayers as they apply to you and your wife.

_____

_____

_____

_____

ANSWERS TO PRAYER

As the spiritual battle of idol-smashing rages, how has the Lord answered your prayers in both you and your wife?

Date: _____ Answer: _____

_____

Date: _____ Answer: _____

_____

Date: _____ Answer: _____

_____

Date: _____ Answer: _____

_____

DAY 30:
GOD-FEARER

PROVERBS 31:30B

A woman who fears the LORD—she shall be praised.

EXPLANATION

Here the author explains that an excellent woman is one who fears the Lord. Such a woman receives praise, as opposed to women who boast only of elegance and beauty, as we read yesterday. Not only does this verse echo the main message of Proverbs,[55] but it also serves as the foundation for all the woman's attributes:

Confidence—She fears the world so little because she fears God so much.

Work ethic—She is so awed by God's work that she desires to represent him in her work.

Grace—She has been embraced by God's grace such that she cannot keep silent about it.

Submission—She submits to her husband because she has first bowed in submission to the Lord.

In his fictional series The Chronicles of Narnia, C. S. Lewis creates a scene where Aslan, the majestic lion and Christ-figure of Narnia, is first mentioned:

> "If there's anyone who can appear before Aslan without their
> knees knocking, they're either braver than most or else just silly."
>
> "Then he isn't safe?" said Lucy.
>
> "Safe?" said Mr. Beaver. "Don't you hear what Mrs. Beaver
> tells you? Who said anything about safe? 'Course he isn't safe.
> But he's good. He's the King, I tell you."[56]

An excellent woman is one who has met the Savior, the
Lion of Judah,[57] and she has been altered forever. She has
allowed him to invade her heart so that she wants to do his will.
She can stand tall for him because she has first bowed low to
him. She fears him with the greatest awe and respect and
thereby becomes a woman of respect. She loves him with a
passion because he first loved her. She serves him because he
was willing to lay down his life for her.

SUGGESTED PRAYER

1. Father, above all else cause my wife to be a woman who
   fears you, and may her fear of you draw her praise.
2. Lord, help me also to fear you and use me to direct my wife's
   vision to you.

JOURNAL

Write some of your own prayers in the space below.

_____

_____

_____

_____

_____

ANSWERS TO PRAYER

How has the Lord answered your prayers for you and your bride?

Date: _____ Answer: _____

_____

Date: _____ Answer: _____

_____

Date: _____ Answer: _____

_____

Date: _____ Answer: _____

_____

DAY 31: PRAISE

PROVERBS 31:31

*Give to her the fruit of her hands,
and let her works
praise her at the city gates.*

EXPLANATION

This verse serves as the conclusion of the entire passage and as an admonition to husbands. A modern-day maxim says that *behind every great man is a great woman*. In this verse, however, the author implies just the opposite: *Behind every great woman is a great man*. The admonition is for the husband to encourage his wife continually in her activities, as she will do far better with his support and encouragement. In other words, a husband should not stifle his wife, but he should delight to see the work of her hands bring her more praise.

Because of the insecurities that lurk deep in all men, however, I have found that many men cannot be excited, or even supportive, when their wives succeed. How can we as men encourage our wives in their work when we struggle with our own craving for praise? Notice in this verse that the woman receives praise at the city gates. Where else in this chapter are the city gates mentioned? In verse 23. The woman's husband sits as a respected elder at those same city gates. What a tremendous visual image with which to close Proverbs 31. The woman stands at the city gates as the elders of the land rise from their seats and give her applause—and her husband is among them! The praise afforded to the woman is a direct praise to her man also. I can imagine the elders remarking to this man *par excellence*, "Brother, you are a fortunate man to have such a wife." Indeed, he is blessed. He is blessed because he gives his blessing to his wife.

SUGGESTED PRAYER

1. Lord, please use me to encourage my wife. Let her always know that I am her biggest fan.
2. Lord, empower me to give her the support she needs, and help me to be genuinely excited about the praise that comes to her as a result of her own work.
3. Lord, forgive me for allowing my own insecurities to eclipse my wife's praise. Renew my confidence in you and use me to be a blessing to my wife.

JOURNAL

Write some of your own prayers in the space below.

_____

_____

_____

_____

ANSWERS TO PRAYER

How has the Lord answered your prayers as you pray for your wife? When was the last time she received praise from you and/or others?

Date: _____ Answer: _____

_____

Date: _____ Answer: _____

_____

Date: _____ Answer: _____

_____

Date: _____ Answer: _____

_____

STUDY GUIDE

The study guide draws from the themes of the daily readings in this book. I have categorized them under headings so that they might lend themselves to teaching, marriage counseling, men's retreats, etc. Feel free to take this material and adjust it to fit your specific need.

I. SACRIFICE AND SUBMISSION

1. In Ephesians 5:22-33, Paul states that a wife is called to submit to her husband. Submission is not a passive activity. In other words, a woman is not a doormat or a slave. A woman who truly submits to her husband actively supports him in his mission and calling. The very construction of the word *submission* speaks of support: *sub* means under, and *mission* speaks of purpose and vision. One who is "sub-missive" has come under the mission to support it. How, therefore, does a wife fulfill the command to submit? What does it look like?

2. If wives are designed by God to submit to their husbands, as evidenced in the creation of woman as a suitable helper to the man (Genesis 2:19-20), why do they struggle with this issue?

3. Is it ever appropriate for a woman not to submit to her husband?

4. If a woman desires to support her husband in his mission, how do you think she feels (and what might she do) if she does not know what the mission is due to lack of communication, laziness, or ignorance on the part of her husband?

5. As a man, do you have a mission? What is it? Do you have goals (temporal and eternal)? Do you know who you are and where you are going? Do you and your wife discuss these things?

6. In Ephesians 5:22-33, Paul states that a husband is called to sacrifice for his wife. Just as submission is not passive, neither is sacrifice. What does it mean for a husband to sacrifice for his wife in an active manner? Does it mean giving up all decision-making and letting the wife have her way?

7. What things do you think men are supposed to sacrifice? What things are they not supposed to sacrifice?

8. If God has wired men to sacrifice for their wives, why do they struggle with this issue?

9. Understanding that marriage points to Christ and the church, how can a husband and wife, who are sacrificing and submitting, reflect the relationship of Christ and his bride?

10. How does Christ sacrifice for the church in the past, in the present, and in the future?

11. How does the church submit to Christ (both in this life and in the life to come)?

II. SECURITY AND SIGNIFICANCE

1. In Ephesians 5:33, Paul admonishes husbands to love their wives, and he admonishes wives to respect their husbands. This idea can also be expressed as women desiring security and men desiring significance. Where have you seen this to be true?

2. Reflect on a woman's need for security (see also the reading from Day 1). Why do you think God is so concerned with widows and orphans throughout the Scriptures (James 1:27)?

3. What type of security does a woman crave on an emotional level? On a physical level? On a spiritual level?

4. How is a man built to meet a woman's desire for security?

5. How does a man crave significance on an emotional level? On a physical level? On a spiritual level?

6. How is a woman built to meet a man's need for significance?

7. What is the difference between the movies and books that women like as opposed to the books and movies that men like? Does this give you insight into the differences between men and women?

8. Consider this diagram demonstrating the healthy cycle where a husband and wife fulfill each other's greatest needs:

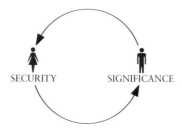

SECURITY   SIGNIFICANCE

9. How does a woman want (or need) to be pursued, rescued, and made to feel safe? How is a man made to pursue and rescue her?

10. What makes a man feel significant? How can his wife make him feel significant?

11. When a woman is made to feel insecure, the tendency is for her to withhold respect. Conversely, when a man is made to feel insignificant, the tendency is for him to withhold love

or to disengage. Thus a vicious cycle can result. Consider the diagram below where a husband and wife fulfill each other's greatest fears:

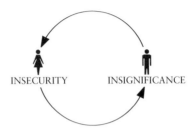

INSECURITY   INSIGNIFICANCE

12. As was stated in question 11, a woman's sinful defense mechanism is to withhold respect. How does she manifest this (actively and passively)? What does this do to her husband?

13. If a woman is not feeling secure in her marriage, how else (or where else) might she wrongly seek security?

14. A man's sinful defense mechanism is to withhold love. How does he manifest this (actively and passively)? What does this do to his wife?

15. If a man is not feeling significant in his marriage, how else (or where else) might he wrongly turn for significance?

16. How is the vicious cycle broken? Put bluntly, how can a woman respect a man who doesn't seem worthy of respect? And how can a man love a woman who isn't lovable? (See reading from Day 5: Rewards. Also consider the overall message of Paul to the Ephesians, especially chapter 2).

17. How does a couple's desire for security and significance point to Christ and his bride? How does Christ provide secu-

rity for the church? How does the church rightly give to Christ the significant place he deserves?

III. PHYSICAL AND SPIRITUAL

1. Have you ever considered the sensual language of the Bible? The Song of Solomon is clear, as are the prophets Isaiah, Jeremiah, and Ezekiel, where God compares the unfaithfulness of his children to spiritual adultery. But consider John 17:20-26, for example, where Christ talks about being *in* us. This should not be surprising since intimate relationships are only to be enjoyed in the context of a covenant.

2. In the physical covenant of a husband and wife, there is penetration, deposit of seed, and ultimate fertilization. Interestingly enough, one of the Hebrew words for male is *zakar*, which comes from the verb to pierce, and one of the Hebrew words for female is *neqeba*, which means to be pierced. The physical picture is self-evident. How, though, does a husband penetrate his wife's soul, character, and heart? (See also entry from Day 3: Trust.)

3. Just as a man wants to be in his wife on a physical level, so also Christ wants to be in his bride on a spiritual level (see John 17:23). Consider the parallels:

Penetration: Christ coming into his church: Revelation 3:20 (we teach our children to ask Christ to come into their hearts).

Deposit of seed: The Word of Christ is likened to seed that is spread to germinate in our lives: Mark 4:1-20.

Fertilization: God desires that the Word of Christ might take root within us and produce fruit: John 15:1-17.

4. How should these insights transform the way we view

worship, prayer, and participation in the sacraments (the most intimate things we can do in the church)?

5. If these insights seem crude, it is because our culture has perverted physical intimacy. How can Christians help restore the glory and sacredness of the physical union?

6. Many churches tell men to suppress their sexuality and masculinity. Not only is this wrong and impossible; it is also not biblical. How can men express their masculinity according to God's design without crossing over into the realm of sin? (See also Day 29: Idol-smasher.)

7. In a parallel fashion, many churches tell women to suppress their sexuality and femininity. This too is wrong, impossible, and not biblical. How can women express their femininity according to God's design without crossing over into the realm of sin?

8. In the context of fidelity, how can the church be unfaithful to Christ?

9. Couples who have never been guilty of an extramarital affair can still be guilty of unfaithfulness. What are other areas where a husband can be unfaithful to his wife, and vice versa?

10. Can you think of other parallels between the earthly covenant of a husband and wife and the spiritual covenant between Christ and his church?

NOTES

1. F. Brown, S. R. Driver, and C. A. Briggs, *A Hebrew and English Lexicon of the Old Testament*, abridged (Oxford: Clarendon Press, 1907).
2. Cf. Matthew 28:20; John 14:1-21; Hebrews 13:5-6.
3. 1 Corinthians 11:3.
4. Ephesians 5:25.
5. Throughout the Old Testament, this Hebrew word for "trust" is always presented in the negative when used in the context of trusting in human relationships, communicating that trust in man (or nations) is a false security. The same word, however, is always used in the positive when referring to trusting in God as the only sure foundation. Proverbs 31:11 is the only exception, making this type of trust dangerous but also commendable. R. Laird Harris, Gleason L. Archer, Jr., and Bruce K. Waltke, *Theological Wordbook of the Old Testament,* Vol. 1 (Chicago, Ill.: Moody Press, 1980), p. 102.
6. Ephesians 5:25.
7. Proverbs 27:17.
8. A woman who truly submits to her husband actively supports him in his mission and calling. The very construction of the word *submission* speaks of support: *sub* means under, and *mission* speaks of purpose and vision. One who is sub-missive is one who has come under the mission to give support.
9. Genesis 2:18.
10. Brother Lawrence, *The Practice of the Presence of God* (Grand Rapids, Mich.: Baker Book House, 1958), pp. 90-91.
11. In 2005 women realtors outnumbered male realtors by 54 percent in full-time employment and 59 percent part-time (statistics taken from www.realtor.org).
12. The average woman abhors the old adage: "It's not personal; it's business." This phrase strikes at the very core of most women, who have a lot to teach us men about the value of a relationship, especially as it applies in business.
13. This word in 31:16 (*considers* or *devises*) is "used mainly of the Lord carrying out his purposes in judgment against the wicked nations or of wicked men who devise schemes against God and the righteous. . . . The book of Proverbs contains the broadest range of meaning relative to this term. There is a sharp division between the negative concept of 'men who devise evil' and the positive notion of 'discretion.' . . . The verb [form] occurs only twice, in Proverbs, once with the normal meaning of 'plot' (Prov 30:32), and once in the sense of 'consider' (31:16). This latter meaning is found in the epilogue of the book, a poem honoring the woman who exemplifies wisdom at its best.

This excellent wife 'considers a field and buys it.' Instead of spending her time dreaming up wicked schemes, she makes plans that will bring great benefit to her family." Harris, Archer, and Waltke, *Theological Wordbook of the Old Testament*, Vol. 1 (Chicago, Ill.: Moody Press, 1980), pp. 244-245.

14. Matthew 28:18-20.
15. Ephesians 5:25-27; Revelation 21:2; 1 Peter 2:9.
16. John 21:15-19.
17. 2 Corinthians 5:11-21.
18. 2 Corinthians 2:15.
19. Craig Van Gelder, *The Essence of the Church, A Community Created by the Spirit* (Grand Rapids, Mich.: Baker Books, 2000), p. 83.
20. Andrew Dornenburg and Karen Page, *Culinary Artistry* (New York: Van Nostrand Reinhold, a division of International Thomson Publishing Company, 1996).
21. Stephen Baldwin, "Redemption's Story," *Charlotte Observer*, November 14, 2004, 6K.
22. John 4:34.
23. Henri Nouwen, *The Wounded Healer* (New York: Image Books, Doubleday, 1972), p. 89.
24. Luke 4:18-19.
25. Genesis 3:21.
26. John 13:3.
27. Edmund Clowney, *The Church* (Downers Grove, Ill.: InterVarsity Press, 1995), pp. 62-63.
28. Isaiah 61:10.
29. Genesis 1:28; Ephesians 5:22-33.
30. A man's sense of a lack of significance is a leading cause in extramarital affairs and midlife crises. A man who feels insignificant at home (due to his wife's lack of respect or from her henpecking) might sinfully seek significance from another source—a secretary or co-worker, which can lead to an affair, or an addiction to work, which can lead to workaholism. This does not excuse a man for such actions, but it does help to explain them.
31. Genesis 1:27.
32. Galatians 3:26—4:7.
33. Isaiah 42:6; 49:6.
34. Out of Israel would come God's anointed Messiah, who would eventually draw all nations to Zion (Isaiah 66:18-24).
35. C. John Miller, *Outgrowing the Ingrown Church* (Grand Rapids, Mich.: Zondervan, 1986), p. 55.
36. *The New International Dictionary of the Bible* (Grand Rapids, Mich.: Zondervan, 1963), p. 590.

37. 2 Samuel 12:24.

38. 2 Samuel 11:2.

39. 2 Samuel 11:8-9.

40. Matthew 1:6.

41. In contrast, one of the most unattractive things to a man is a woman who is ill-tempered, fretful, and quarrelsome (Proverbs 21:19; 25:24).

42. See Proverbs 3.

43. Proverbs 9:13.

44. See also James 3:1-12.

45. Titus 2:11-14.

46. Throughout the Scriptures, various types of figurative bread are mentioned: The bread of the land (Numbers 15:19); bread of affliction (Deuteronomy 16:3); bread of wickedness (Proverbs 4:17), etc. In these cases, bread is either the product of something (like the land, implying what the land yields as food) or something in which one indulges or has been given to eat (like the bread of wickedness).

47. Henry Fairlie, *The Seven Deadly Sins Today* (Notre Dame, Ind.: University of Notre Dame Press, 1979), p. 129.

48. Philippians 2:4.

49. Ephesians 5:28-33.

50. Consider this passage from Proverbs 30:21-23 where we are given the picture of an unappreciated woman (italics mine): "Under three things the earth trembles; under four it cannot bear up: a slave when he becomes king, and a fool when he is filled with food; *an unloved woman when she gets a husband*, and a maidservant when she displaces her mistress."

51. Ephesians 2:8-10; Titus 3:4-8.

52. Eugene Peterson, *Five Smooth Stones for Pastoral Work* (Grand Rapids, Mich.: Eerdmans, 1980), pp. 64-65.

53. In Hebrew the word is *emptiness*, the same word that the author of Ecclesiastes used when he wrote, "Vanity of vanities, says the Preacher, vanity of vanities! All is vanity" (Ecclesiastes 1:2).

54. Bruce Marshall, *The World, the Flesh and Father Smith* (Boston, Mass.: Houghton Mifflin, 1945), p. 108.

55. Proverbs 1:7: "The fear of the LORD is the beginning of knowledge; fools despise wisdom and instruction."

56. C. S. Lewis, *The Lion, the Witch and the Wardrobe* (New York: Collier Books, 1950), pp. 75-76.

57. Revelation 5:5.

BIBLIOGRAPHY

Brother Lawrence. *The Practice of the Presence of God with Spiritual Maxims*. Grand Rapids, Mich.: Spire Books, 1958.

Brown, F., Driver, S. R., and Briggs, C. A. *A Hebrew and English Lexicon of the Old Testament (abridged)* (Based on *A Hebrew and English Lexicon of the Old Testament*, by F. Brown, S. R. Driver, and C. A. Briggs. Oxford: Clarendon Press, 1907. Digitized and abridged as a part of the Princeton Theological Seminary Hebrew Lexicon Project under the direction of Dr. J. M. Roberts. Used by permission. Electronic text corrected, formatted, and hypertexted by OakTree Software, Inc., 2001).

Chapell, Bryan. *Christ-Centered Preaching*. Grand Rapids, Mich.: Baker Books, 1994.

_____. *Each for the Other, Marriage As It's Meant to Be*. Grand Rapids, Mich.: Baker Books, 1998.

Clowney, Edmund P. *The Church*, from the commentary series Contours of Christian Theology. Downers Grove, Ill.: InterVarsity Press, 1995.

Doriani, Daniel. *The Life of a God-made Man, Becoming a Man After God's Heart*. Wheaton, Ill.: Crossway Books, 2001.

Dornenburg, Andrew, and Page, Karen. *Culinary Artistry*. New York: Van Nostrand Reinhold, a division of International Thomson Publishing, 1996.

Dostoevsky, Fyodor. *The Brothers Karamazov*. Trans. Andrew H. MacAndrew. New York: Bantam Books, Inc., 1970.

Douglas, J. D., and Tenney, Merrill C. *The New International Dictionary of the Bible*. Grand Rapids, Mich.: Zondervan Publishing House, 1963.

Fairlie, Henry. *The Seven Deadly Sins Today*. Notre Dame, Ind.: University of Notre Dame Press, 1979.

BIBLIOGRAPHY

Feyerabend, Karl. *Langenscheidt's Pocket Hebrew Dictionary to the Old Testament, Hebrew-English*. Maspeth, N.Y.: Langenscheidt Publishers, n.d.

Harris, R. Laird, Archer, Gleason L., Jr., and Waltke, Bruce K. *Theological Wordbook of the Old Testament*, Vols. 1 and 2. Chicago, Ill.: Moody Bible Institute, 1980.

Lewis, C. S. *Till We Have Faces*. Orlando, Fla.: Harcourt Brace Jovanovich, 1957.

_____. *The Lion, the Witch and the Wardrobe*. New York: Collier Books, 1950.

Miller, C. John. *Outgrowing the Ingrown Church*. Grand Rapids, Mich.: Zondervan Publishing House, 1986.

Nouwen, Henri J. M. *The Wounded Healer*. New York: Doubleday, 1979.

Peterson, Eugene. *Five Smooth Stones for Pastoral Ministry*. Grand Rapids, Mich.: Eerdmans Publishing Co., 1980.

Van Gelder, Craig. *The Essence of the Church, A Community Created by the Spirit*. Grand Rapids, Mich.: Baker Books, 2000.

Willard, Dallas. *Renovation of the Heart, Putting on the Character of Christ*. Colorado Springs, Colo.: NavPress, 2002.